Tears of

Broken Hearts

Cover Design: TreManda Pewett
Editor: Carla DuPont Huger & Sarah Plamondon
Illustration: TreManda Pewett

ISBN 13: **978-1-949191-13-4**

Tears of
Broken Hearts

Pierre Alex Jeanty

Disclaimer

This book was first published under my pen name L. Figaro.

Table of Contents

Becoming yours...

Pierre A. Jeanty

Warning

Over the years,

I have learned that some relationships are

unattended wells people fall into.

They injure themselves as they drop,

giving birth to invisible scars as the darkness at

the bottom makes it harder to recognize

themselves.

They fight not to drown with hope that

someone else will make a bucket out of their

own heart, and let it down for them to fight their

way up to the light.

I just climbed my way out of one of those wells

not too long ago, but don't worry, I've had

plenty of time to think and be my own savior

expecting no one else's heart to come save me.

Funny

What's funny

is that I used to laugh at the thought

of growing any feelings for you.

There was never enough soil, I thought.

Little did I know that the thought was planted

and slowly it was watered.

Here we are,

I am more than interested in you,

and you are the apple of my eyes.

<u>*Hesitant*</u>

I am not afraid of love one bit.

Love and I shared some beautiful experiences

despite the ugly hearts

I tried to harvest it in.

I still believe that beautiful hearts fly freely,

like butterflies looking for flowers to rest on.

I am still trying to figure

if I am the flower or the butterfly.

Love comes

My heart:

If we are being honest,

I do not feel worthy of love for the most part.

I'm slowly opening my arms to welcome it,

though I have had enough wounds to believe it

is not my friend.

My mind:

I am learning that love doesn't attach itself to

anything with hate's sponsorship.

I am now understanding those who came and

assassinated my heart weren't hitmen hired by

love, but false disciples I made my messiah.

Me:

So, love, if you find my number,

please wait until after the third ring.

<u>*Walk*</u>

You caught me at an unexpected moment

and quite unusually,

you didn't allow me to fall to catch me.

You kept me from falling by grabbing my hand,

asking me to walk in love with you.

This was our beginning.

Courting

Your outdated gestures
made our dates feel like never-ending holidays.
If this is what I should expect love to be,
I am more than willing to be a fool for it.

Preparation

Love songs after love songs

I demanded my ears to swallow,

trying to cleanse my emotions of resentment.

This temple must be ready,

if it wants this new love to grow old here.

More than I asked God for

All this time I've been searching for my star,

but little did I know

I would meet an entire universe.

The first

Everything about meeting you

the first time was convincing.

You had me at our first conversation.

I remember going home,

missing both of your pink lips

and the words that ran from them.

Full package

You're a sealed envelope

with everything good

I have never known,

and a pinch of the bad that

I have never seen but wondered about.

You have your own stamp of approval

and your priorities don't need to be addressed.

I cannot see how a maturing love

could not find roots between us.

Nerds

Few people know how to

keep a great conversation,

and fewer people know how to

keep my mind challenged.

Our conversations became consistent

at doing both.

That's how you stole my body and soul;

you penetrated my mind.

I don't usually do this

Your presence became my favorite gift.

How easily I was influenced

to unwrap myself slowly,

exposing you to all the surprise that comes

wrapped up in this flesh.

Belong

We belong together,

like oxygen belongs in our lungs,

like angels belong on this earth,

like heaven belongs in our hearts.

Dreams come true

The softness of your skin became beautiful

sheets

for me to fall asleep on and dream.

Your chest became my pillow with love songs

at the edge of its lips.

<u>Resting</u>

I love the way you bury your head

in the surface of my chest.

You find comfort here,

and I find it comforting that you do;

it's heartwarming.

While you're here,

I hope your ears hear the love songs

my heart is singing because of you.

Numbers game

I've met plenty who could be the *1*

and looked like perfect *10*s.

They never saw *2* as a beautiful number,

but loved in *3*s and *sometimes* more.

You however, look like *1* I can count on.

Effort

Your series of morning texts,

Your online posts about me,

Your snap chat of us,

Your late-night calls...

all created an excitement in me

that will not die any time soon.

This fire burns differently.

You caught me

I no longer have to
fall in love with the idea
of falling in love with someone like you.

Addictive

You are easily the strongest person

I've ever met.

Easier than that is my weakness for you.

You've become a craving

that will never find its way out of me.

I long to be yours each day,

more than I long to see tomorrow.

Protection

Your love has become a band
that surrounds the boundaries of my heart,
making sure the broken pieces never come

apart.

Halfway commitment

I knew I had to hang on to you
when you showed me that
seeing commitment as a noose,
is only for those who do not have
a good head on their shoulders.

Love rat

You looked at me with eyes of hope;
behind them I saw hunger racing inside
like a lab rat in its exercise ball.

I am praying that my love will be enough
and that your hunger will eventually
find its way out,
instead of moving and going nowhere.

<u>Mr. & Mrs.</u>

I've never been more
than titles with anyone else.

<u>*A life of love*</u>

You held me like a dying person

trying to hold on to life.

If I am honest,

I live to see moments like this.

Love crossing

We are more than lovers;

we are soul mates who swam through

lakes of hurt,

rivers of pain,

and oceans of disappointment

to find one another.

Hollywood

One day I wanted to tell you that I've

never been loved like this...

but then

I realized that I've never been loved.

This love

I've only seen on the television screen,

but nowhere else.

Feels like a movie.

Lovers and friends

Lovers turn into friends quite often.

This was the first time I've had

a friend become a lover.

Usually I fall for them,

we become lovers,

and everything ends too soon

because we can't find a way to build a

friendship,

the most important part of love.

A night out

I've come to realize that you and I

are two people who want to be made love to

before the sky is dark,

at the fair,

on a Ferris wheel,

with our clothes on.

Smile

I can watch you smile for days,

and even eternity.

It's such a beautiful curve.

Heaven must be somewhere

between your left and right cheeks.

Melody

Some have told you that you talk too much,

or not soft enough.

Maybe I am too in love to realize any of this,

but at this point,

music to my ears is any sound that climbs

out of your mouth.

Your voice has become my favorite song.

<u>Due</u>

I feel my heart kicking inside my chest

when I say,

"I don't know if I'm ready."

It knows I'm lying and that I've been pregnant

with love for years.

My Angel

You made life the easiest

during my hardest days,

and brought me light

during the darkest nights.

I am convinced that your touch can end wars

and even convince the devil to apologize,

and attempt to reclaim his place

with God once again.

A "she" poem

Every cell in my body sees nothing wrong

with cellulite on yours.

I am not one of those boys

who glorify altered beauty;

you've altered my life far too much for me to

be blinded by things that will not last forever.

Nothing on that body of yours

will be shamed by me.

When my lips touch yours,

when my compliments greet your ears,

when my hands rest on your skin,

I am feeling more than attraction.

I am seeing more than a body.

I am falling in love with your soul.

<u>Connected</u>

"I feel like an open book around you,"

you said.

"Does this mean

your heart is holding hands with mine,

and they are skipping to their own beats?"

I asked.

You smiled.

<u>I'm yours</u>

Love me in a way that is

unwelcoming to my insecurities,

a way that closes the door in the face of fear,

and trust me in a way that lets doubt ring

the doorbell without an answer.

But

This skin is like a blanket;

I wash it,

dry it,

and use it to keep my heart warm

from this world.

On some nights

I am comfortable under it,

yet on other days I toss and turn and feel

as if I am lying on cactus.

Falling

I have never done this before.

Never have I let myself fall in love

this deeply

without a parachute.

Take it slow

I know to take things slow,

but I am clueless on how to

make my heart move

at a slower pace when it comes to you.

You've become weak to your knees for me

and I can't stand being without you.

How can I not dive heart first?

Exploration

I used to want to travel the world.

I still do,

and would want to do it with you.

But even more so,

there's nothing I'd rather do than search out

every piece of land in your soul,

every mountain,

and the rivers your tears come from.

I am eager to navigate through every part of

you.

Muse

Those who have seen God

cannot be convinced out of their religion.

This is why I am a poet.

How could I see both simplicity and complexity

dancing in the same room

and not grab a brush and my canvas?

Piece by piece

The beauty in us is that we do not

aspire to fix each other.

Our only goal is to be the missing piece

for each other's puzzle.

Two-gether

Together we are what the old wish

they would've become,

and what the young aspire to be.

Let's let our love grow like the old,

while we keep it young.

The One

If we last,

You'll be the first.

To be honest,

I am praying that you are the one

who removes the hopeless out of

my hopelessly romantic soul.

Pierre A. Jeanty

Honeymoon...

Pierre A. Jeanty

Honey

The love gurus call it the honeymoon stage.

I am stuck on how sweet you taste to me,

and how you light up the darkest corners of my

heart.

Unreal

In you was buried a love that
I've been trying to dig out of
the dead relationships,
with people who believed love to be
a ghost they had seen.

Need you

I became your child,

searching for life in you.

You have become a necessity to my survival.

Wait a minute

How can you see the good

when you only want to find bad?

How can you walk away when

you haven't stayed long enough?

Leaving can't be the solution this early.

These are just problems we haven't solved.

Open

I was longing for validation,

and you parked your beautiful words

on the driveway of my mind,

right outside my heart.

The next thing I knew,

I wasn't handing you keys to unlock the doors;

I drove through my own walls,

forcing a way for you to come in.

Leasing

Somehow you silenced the voice of my

insecurity

with your flowery words,

reassuring eyes,

and warming hand gestures.

My heart can't help but

make itself a home for you now,

rather than a rental property of which

the landlord waits on the happiness

agreement to end,

and put a new tenant in with better promises.

<u>*Yours truly*</u>

I am not falling into love,

but into you.

It's not you I fell for,

but your heart that caught mine.

Making mountains

They say those who don't argue much
are in trouble because there's not
enough care in them to fight.
When we aren't fighting,
it only looks like we care for each other...
Maybe we are normal.
Maybe we aren't at all,
and we are brushing far too many
issues to the side,
unwilling to jeopardize our sense of happiness.

Cloud 9

Some of my friends say you are not it for me

and that my head is in the clouds.

The screams from the zombies of

their failed relationships make it hard

for me to hear them out.

Hero

I will continue to caress the mask

until you grow enough courage to

show me the face behind it.

Idolizing

I fell further into you,

then I fell out of myself and out of God's hand.

Somehow you became my god,

lording over every part of me,

becoming the savior

I could not live without.

Reassuring

You told me that the word beautiful
never crossed paths with your name,
and that the girls in the media made it easy
for you to see why.
Right then and there I reminded you
that those girls don't get to show the face
they were born with,
but the face the marketing directors
chose to show the consumer.

The missing piece

You did not complete me,

you added to me.

I had wings before you,

but you gave me enough reasons to fly.

Denial

Your shortcomings only signify that
you have not arrived to a place
where you'd like to be.
We all are unfinished products packed
and delivered into this world.

Finding my way

You're the ocean drowning within itself.

Worth so much,

yet feeling worthless.

I am not here to change that,

but I am here to scuba dive

until I explore every part of you.

There are too many things for me to love about

you that you don't love about yourself.

Because of you

You gave me reasons to dig for the beauty

that is planted in this world.

What happened?

Slowly you are showing me

the ugliness that

has also grown roots here.

Unanswered

You've proven that you are not like the others.

You've loved me differently;

you've touched me, kissed me,

hugged me in ways

they never knew could be done.

I see the similarities swimming in your actions

and slowly merging themselves into your

speech.

But how can it be?

This honeymoon has been far too beautiful

to divorce from it.

Handle it

Long were the days we danced around
our problems while we held hands in silence,
hoping we would hop over our issues
and leave it to love to ask forgiveness.
Soon enough we learned that forgiveness
cannot do its job without a hand from us.

What are we?

We are the sum total of good

flirting with bad;

multiple heartbreaks mislead us, coming in

between and dividing us

to take away from our love story.

We aren't just numbers,

let's not become another statistic written about

unhealthy relationships.

Time will tell

Here we are,

fighting like everyone else.

Everyone fights for different reasons,

some for the good and some for nothing.

Eventually we will see if we are good,

or nothing.

I needed you

You cannot remain the sun

when night comes for a season into my life.

You must be my moon.

During the darkness,

I need light more than I need to hear

complaints about why I am changing.

Fight

I am not blind,

but deaf to the voices

telling me to let go.

You don't build to withstand,

you only stop building once

you feel like you're done.

Well, death isn't here yet.

Wonders

Maybe suicide is me being in love with you.

Maybe insanity is me being here,

while reasons for me to leave continue to build

their pyramid for the world to see.

Were you even different?

Trying to hold onto you is starting to be
like trying to hold on to water.
I've cupped my hands to make your heart
more comfortable,
but you continue to toss and turn,
letting me know that you do not
find rest here anymore.
It's sad,
I am watching us reach the point
I've reached with everyone else.

All coming into the light

When I found myself praising you

for the things lovers ought to do

and begging you for things

lovers ought to give,

that is when I realized

that our fire was dying out.

Pierre A. Jeanty

The beginning

of the end...

Countdown

People change every day.

Why did our change have to mean the end?

Burden

I cannot carry your baggage for you,

I can only grab a handle,

walk with you,

and be there to help you unload it.

I wish you could've seen this before we took off.

Running out of ink

When I couldn't talk to you,

I talked to my pages about you.

My pen bled and bled,

while I cried and cried.

Slowly burning

Our heaven became hell.
We sat in the pain,
wallowing in uncertainty,
tormented by each other's fire.
Yet, we stayed to watch
everything we built crash,
burning into ashes.

Neglect

You held gifts and beautiful remarks
against my mouth when I tried to open it
to ask for what I deserved.

It's not a game

When you tried to treat me like an option,

I audibled out.

You don't get it.

I am speaking football while you are searching

for sounds in my voice.

Nothing I ever said traveled through the right

direction into your ears.

Maybe this is why we are here.

Hands on the stove

You were a wildfire contained by flesh.

I was mesmerized by your flames,

they excited me.

I argued with people who said

you were dangerous,

as you moved in slowly.

You were melting my cold heart.

How could you be so dangerous, I thought.

Until the adrenaline stopped,

I didn't realize how much of me was burnt.

Today

I should've let go of you yesterday.

But today, I am apologizing to tomorrow

just in case it becomes another yesterday that

sings the same tune as the others.

Month after month

When your absence became a holiday

I often celebrated,

it was then I started talking about us in

numbers,

counting down the calendar days.

Where's love?

I've been yearning to make love,

but you taunt me to give you sex.

Our bodies are always rubbing against

each other,

but we never see the fire.

We are losing our spark,

but you can't see that.

As long as your lustful needs are fulfilled,

you remain blind to my need for love.

Things change

Your "_I love you_" slowly changed from being

a reminder that I am loved,

to a reminder that every lie carries

a little truth on its back.

Privacy isn't secrecy

We were the sun and the moon holding hands.

Your love only shined for me in the dark

while mine was for the world to see in the

daytime.

Bad fruits

Disobedience may have been the act that

caused Adam to be stripped from the soil of

Eden,

but blame was the transgression that sealed

their eviction letter from God.

Look how we still carry that curse.

You do what you know you shouldn't do,

yet blame me.

Fine

We ended our conversations with, *"I'm fine,"*

when not a single thing was fine with us.

Your *"fine,"* was a period keeping an overrun

sentence from flooding from your tongue.

My *"fine,"* was,

"How many times am I going to be pulled over

for my speeding mouth, outrunning my

thoughts by speaking things that are unlawful?"

We aren't fine, we are only finding our way

out of this love affair.

More than the eyes can see

We never laid hands on each other,

but we sure knew how to

throw punches with our words.

We look so healthy,

yet so bruised emotionally.

No flicker

Your trust slipped through my fingers,

landing into the pit of your lies.

In torment rested our love story, lifeless.

We cannot rekindle things like this,

this fire has been put out far too many times to

ever ignite once again.

Yolo

You said you were just living a little,
having some fun,
because a relationship should not make
anyone a disciple of boredom.
That was all true,
but that truth became the knife that cut me
to every song the DJ played at that party.

You put the blame on drinking,
yet those shots called you a liar.
The alcohol says it is only your therapist who
occasionally brings out the real you
to play in the light.
Here I am sitting in the dark,
wondering what hints I missed
in your behaviors.

Red cycles

I am good at recognizing stop signs,

but terrible at seeing red flags.

Stop signs are a matter of life and death at

times and red flags,

Well they are a matter of love or death.

Perhaps when love is involved,

my emotions make it hard to see,

so I blindly love hoping that their eyes will open

up and love me.

I tend to rely solely on my impaired vision,

and it leads me to see things I don't want to

see.

Gone with the wind

You became my hero.

When in danger,

you showed up while I struggled under piles

of terrible promises,

almost lifeless.

You rescued me, covering me with your own

promises that were far more promising.

I became obsessed with your special skills,

you wonder woman.

As I continued to be made safe by you,

I wondered if you'd ever wander away.

I know now.

False hope

Even when your lies became as clear as the sky,

I still searched for the sunshine in you,

wishing your clouds would only

rain truth one of these days.

Hurricane...

I've experienced hurricanes before;
they destroy cities and leave homes damaged.
I wonder if the people chosen to name them,
name them after lovers who damaged their
hearts
and destroyed their ideas of love.

You swept through this temple with all
categories of words,
pouring and ripping through the bones that are
meant to be walls keeping this hope of mine
safe.

You've caused my eyes to flood
far too many times.
I hope one is named after you one day.

Silence speaks

I once believed that what you said hurt us,

but I think I am wrong about that.

It is what was not said

that I believe destroyed us.

The unsaid became the evil who hired

assumption

as the hitman

to gun down our future.

Our love died trying to fill in the blank of the

silence.

Throwing stones

Your insecurities had their way

of showing themselves.

They loudly exposed mine,

and used their dirty fingers to point at me.

Directions

Could it be that our relationship
was just an intersection rather than
two parallel lanes merging into one?

Her & I

The fact that we overcame the world together

convinced me to keep you in my world much

longer. That is how I began believing

that we were Bonnie and Clyde; sure enough,

everything we did robbed us of a less-broken

future.

Seasonal

You changed like the seasons,

becoming winter

while I was starting to spring

out of my fear of love.

How do I keep falling for love that sounds like

forever, but only last the summer?

<u>Misinterpreted</u>

Why do you find threat in my words,

knives in my sentences,

and bullets in my tone?

Nothing I do is ever right to you,

all while I am the one being truly wronged.

You carelessly cut me with every word,

yet find even my softest response to be

anger pounding on your ear drums.

How can we stay in love like this

when I am not being loved, and

you find reason to say my love isn't enough?

Nonsense

If I loved you the way you claimed to love me,

would you still remain blind?

Would you still be deaf

to the sound of my needs?

Would you still act so tastelessly

and be void of feelings?

Would you still carry the smell of betrayal

on your body?

I can't help but wonder,

would you even come to your senses?

What is left of us

We are more than bridges burned.

We are the ashes of two continents.

Sun & Moon

As long as earth continues to rotate,

meeting you will be like an eclipse.

Wasn't meant to be

The person who stole your heart was not a thief,

they were simply in it for the reward.

You can't steal what you were given.

Nor are they home wreckers;

how do you wreck a home that is without a

foundation?

Strange

I used to carry thoughts about us tying the knot,

but now I only feel knots in my stomach when

my eyes are forced to recognize your existence.

How strange it is to me that

we never truly progressed.

We started as strangers,

and ended up estranged.

The blind misjudge

You say, _"Who am I to judge?"_

while you toy with my fragile heart.

You condemn feelings I have only for you,

although you misled me to this destination.

I've heard people say,

"Only God can judge me," as a defense,

but never as an escape route to avoid

having their wrongs accounted for.

If choosing not to ignore the obvious makes me

a judge, then I will not change my verdict.

You are guilty.

I am not the only one

Some people cannot get over the fact

that their lovers have slept with people before

them.

I, on the other hand,

am trying to get over the fact that

you never stopped while with me.

Emotional

These waves of emotions are nothing new,

they are merely signs that my heart

is drowning from believing that

you were a life jacket.

All my eggs went into your basket,

and now my life is scrambled with

the coldest burn I've ever felt.

<u>It's no one else's fault</u>

They did not owe me an ounce of royalty,

but perhaps a little respect for our relationship.

They may have led you to

their embrace and seduced you,

but the royalty was yours only to pay.

They may have been the perfect temptation,

but you committed the sin.

I will not grow angry at them one bit,

You were the lousy guard not responsible

enough

to protect my heart.

Feelings change, love doesn't

You say that I have changed,
and that is why you cannot find a way to
continue being in love with me.
I watch you says these things,
with no make-up on,
a little more overweight,
with a less paying job than before,
and a sharper tongue.
You didn't stay the same,
and my feelings simply never changed.

Pierre A. Jeanty

Revelation...

Pierre A. Jeanty

Let's get this straight

The poems I write about you are not for you.

I am not reliving us.

I am emptying myself by pouring

the residue of _you_ onto paper.

<u>*Missing you*</u>

I don't think I miss you nearly as much
as my phone misses those morning texts
from your number.

Love lasts forever

Everyone who has fallen in love

has caught a glimpse of forever.

The fortunate ones are those who look back on

it

as both of their lives draw close to the end,

rather than those who only saw it alive

at the beginning of it all.

<u>Fighting</u>

"Are you O.K.?" they ask, investigating with the
purest intent.
"Yes I am," I reply, while every single part of
me wants to scream, *"No!"*
I've wrestled with the thought
of you being gone,
the thought of what we had
never being anything,
the thought of never finding anyone
trustworthy.
I am not O.K.
I am K.O.'ed.

It shows

You're not the only one who pretends

not to miss what we had.

The difference between us

is that I am the weaker one,

and still haven't built my appetite

for new love.

Neglected child

I tried to find inside of you,
the love I sought from those who
brought me into this world.

Nothing to hide

There are those who mourn the death

of their relationship by draining

themselves of the feelings,

and those who turn and run into different

relationships and different beds.

I am one of those who let it hurt,

let the tears fall,

and let the pain show.

I may have been fooled,

but at least I know that I have loved and fought.

I did it before

It's been months since you left.

The ghost of our relationship is still living

and breathing in my home.

I am the same as I was before,

the oxygen didn't leave me when you left.

I guess I can live without you after all.

Rain

This rain pouring out of my eyes

did not come from the clouds

of sadness and disappointments

that formed when you took sunshine from me.

No, its source is me looking at myself

and realizing how much I mistreated myself

to treat you like royalty.

???

Did you not know that people
who go their separate ways do not easily
separate themselves from their current ways?
I am still purging you out of my habits.

Being close to you burns

After you left, I looked for reasons to go after

you.

I even consulted with the ghost

of your potential that became my comforter.

I could not find one,

yet still I went after you.

In the end,

I had only found reasons to be as far

from you as the sun is from the earth.

Being my own

The only thing I've learned from us being

together,

is that my heart is the safest in my own hands,

when I am loving my own dang self.

<u>No next time</u>

I am now finding the good
that came from you saying goodbye.

The proof is in the pudding

They say people meet for certain reasons,

but I refuse to believe that you were a lesson.

You were the consequence of impulsive

choices.

You came into my life for a reason alright;

as a reminder that becoming drunk in love

should come from sober choices.

<u>Insomnia</u>

You are the reason I sleep during the daytime

to keep the dreams away,

and stay awake at night to keep myself

from reliving the nightmare.

Your everything

In trying to prove to you that
I am more than enough for you,
I found reasons to see myself as
someone who is short of everything.

<u>What are you reaping?</u>

If we are being honest,

I want karma to both make you pay

for your sins against me,

and leave you alone.

I have never judged you,

but I wonder if you'd feel guilty

if you got what you deserved for treating me

with less than I deserved.

The island

And here I am alone,

surrounded by my tears.

I gather the pieces of my heart,

trying to see the bigger picture of

what went wrong.

Was it because I loved you too fast?

Was it because it wasn't meant to be?

I get lost trying to find the answers to feed

my need for closure.

Wondering

Is the person you are saying, "I love you," to,

in for the same reality as me,

or are they getting out of you

what I needed from you?

<u>Prioritizing</u>

I've learned to treat myself as an option as well,

except I am choosing all of the above now.

Me, Myself, and *I* are the choices.

Barhopping

Whiskey, vodka, and rum are not stitches that

pull together the broken pieces of the heart.

They are what sting the cuts,

they are reminders that the pain

needs treatment.

They do not bring healing,

they are temporary band-aids.

<u>*Honesty*</u>

When you tell your friends

about the things I *didn't* do,

please be sure you tell them

about the things you *did* do.

<u>Can't tell me nothing</u>

Don't tell me how I should feel now that
I am trying to drain myself of feelings
that are still breathing for you.
Remember, you told me not to tell you how
your heart should be more open to feel love.

Day by day

I stopped holding on to depression
when I finally let go of you.
I did not do it by will, it was a sacrifice.
I couldn't stand watching my happiness
get choked to death by your presence
resting in my mind.
It was my happiness or you;
I chose my happiness,
and freedom came to rest at my feet.

Exes aren't meant to be friends

Being cordial is not for the mature,

but the healed.

I am still bleeding,

therefore I will not look at you,

showing calmness when we cross paths.

I will be cold,

I will act numb,

I will not speak.

This is how I heal,

by showing how I truly feel about you.

Maybe we can be cordial later on,

but we will never be friends.

Thought you might want to know

I am seeing other people now.

I am seeing if I can see you in them.

You may have made your bed of

"I don't care about you anymore,"

but I know there's still a little curiosity sleeping

underneath those covers of defensiveness.

No more denial

Friends tell me that you are doing
things to make me jealous.
I hope you're not.
If you are, you must know that it will not be
enough to cause my heart to put down the
shovel,
and stop digging this grave.
It is set on digging a hole deep enough to keep
you from climbing out, even if you resurrected.

Unstable

They were my mental illness;

how could that be?

A question only the inconsiderate might ask.

To have the very person hurting you

living in your head,

nothing in you wanting to kick them out,

is torture.

You become bipolar,

one minute drooling

and rejoicing and the next,

eyes leaking and growing angry

at the thought of them.

<u>Caring for you as a person</u>

When we are vulnerable, our desire for
something makes us fall for anything.
I remember hearing a boy say, "*vulnerable girls
coming out of relationships are the easiest.*"
I pray you're not running after his type.
I hope you're not making it easy for anyone
who comes to make a playground out of you,
and leave after recess.

Finding myself

After wrestling with the feeling of

being lost without you,

I finally tapped out.

I found the person the younger me

needed me to be.

_K..._

My long texts hate your short responses.

There's nothing they hate more than

not knowing whether they are meant to be

a fence to keep me out,

or just a reminder that you don't need

anything to keep me out,

because nothing in you wants me to come in.

Forced entries on damage doors

When we force wrong things into

what we believe to be right places,

we break things.

When we force love,

we break our own hearts.

Hopeful

Your absence welcomed the presence of peace

and the warmth of self-love into my life.

I've grown wiser and stronger since we existed.

I will never say that love failed me,

I can only say that the love I found in you

and those who came before you were only

snippets of what is to come.

People in love fail each other almost every time

the sun closes its eyes,

but I know that the love that is meant to be will

find its way to prove us disappointed ones

wrong.

Confirmation

When tomorrow wakes up,

the thought of you will no longer be here.

Our memories will no longer be

too much for me to carry,

and my eyes will no longer allow tears

to make their way down my cheek.

I will feel good about myself,

I will feel good about being alone for a while.

I will feel again.

Waiting

Our love is gone,

but I am waiting to meet love again.

I hope to meet the love that will stay

sooner than later.

Pierre A. Jeanty

THE END...

until new love comes

Other books by Pierre Jeanty

Free Book

Watering Your Soil

Download at **wateringyoursoil.com**

Best Sellers

HER

HER Vol. 2

Ashes of Her Love

Sparking Her Own Flame

Unspoken Feelings of a Gentleman

To the Women I Once Loved

HIM

Other Books

Unspoken Feelings of a Gentleman II

In Love with You

Apologies That Never Came

Really Moving On

Coming soon

HEart

All available at pierrejeanty.com

Pierre A. Jeanty

Made in the USA
Las Vegas, NV
09 February 2021

17514316R10100